Original Title: Meditation Moments

Copyright © 2023 Book Fairy Publishing
All rights reserved.

Editors: Theodor Taimla
Autor: Annabel Swan
ISBN 978-9916-39-439-7

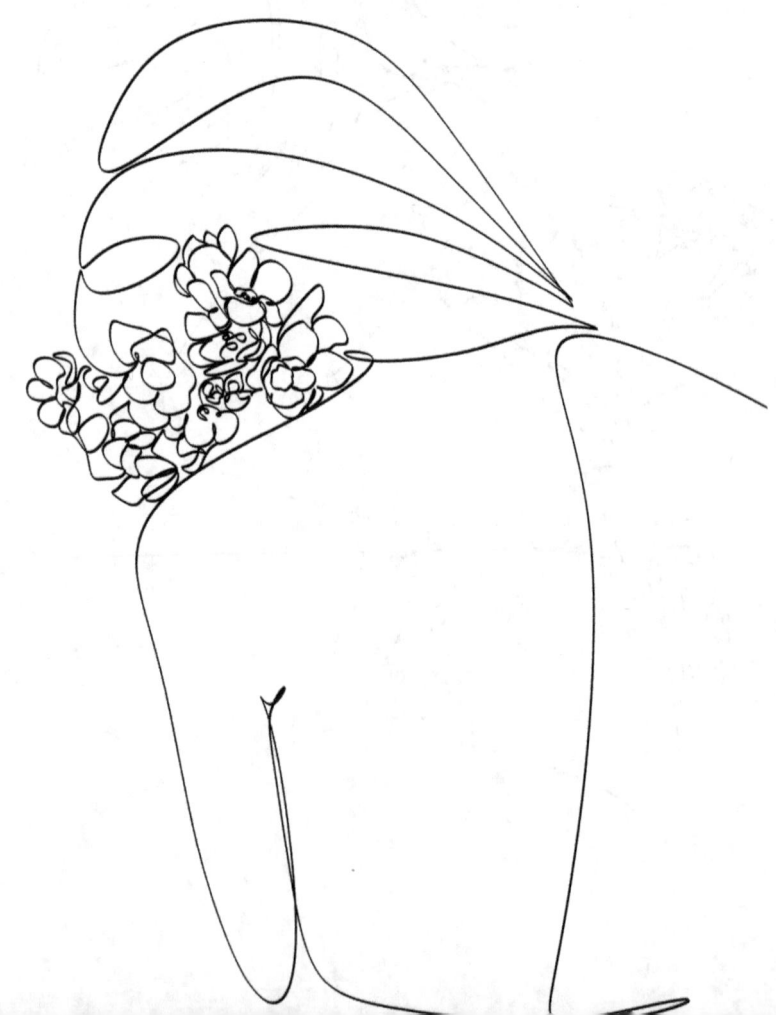

Meditation Moments

Annabel Swan

The Hush Hour

The world retreats, its sounds subside,
As twilight brings the hush hour's tide.
A whispering breeze, the sole voice heard,
While day to night, transitions blurred.

In the hush hour, secrets speak,
Shadows dance, the moonlight's peek.
Stars above, in silence, plot,
To sprinkle dreams that daylight forgot.

A hushed symphony, the night's ensemble,
In its quietude, hearts tremble.
Embrace the calm, the stillness deep,
For in the hush hour, souls seep.

Satori Sunrise

With the first light, horizons wake,
To Satori Sunrise, senses take.
An epiphany in every ray,
Illuminating paths, a new way.

Mind ascends with the daybreak's hues,
In silence, life's essence views.
Bathed in warmth, a mindful kiss,
In this dawn, find your bliss.

Colors blend, a dawning art,
Each one a beat of nature's heart.
Satori Sunrise, a vision clear,
Awakens truth, brings it near.

Stilled Thoughts

In the quiet depth of mind,
Stilled thoughts are there to find.
Beyond the noise, the inner sea,
Calms the soul, sets it free.

Breathe in deep, the moment's hush,
Let go of strife, the world's mad rush.
Eyes closed tight, a journey starts,
Within, explore the silent parts.

In the stillness, understand,
Each thought's an untouched strand.
Weave them gently, peace to induct,
In stilled thoughts, wisdom's construct.

Velvet Reflections

In twilight's hush, a velvet sky,
A canvas deep and wide,
Moon's gentle touch, where stars imply
Eternal dreams collide.

Within the mirror of the night,
Each thought a ripple seems,
A dance of shadows in soft light,
Beneath the cloak of dreams.

Silence speaks in whispered tones,
Through the velvet void,
Reflecting love that time enthrones,
In hearts, not easily destroyed.

Silhouettes of Silence

Quiet moments caught in time,
Silhouettes that softly chime,
Echoes of the silent night,
Hold the world in grayscale light.

Whispers in the evening air,
Secrets that the shadows bear,
Silence drapes its calming shawl,
Over the souls that dare to call.

Figures cast on walls so stark,
Tracing tales within the dark,
Silent forms that bend and dance,
In silence, find their true romance.

Delving Deeper

Beneath the surface, secrets keep,
In hidden vaults that seem to sleep,
Delving deeper, seeking truth,
In the timeless well of youth.

Past the masks that we all wear,
Through the fog of false compare,
Layers peeling one by one,
Until the core is finally won.

There, in depths of inner sight,
Where darkness dares to touch the light,
Understanding starts to steep,
In the soul's deep, endless leap.

Patience in Bloom

Patient petals, poised to swell,
Whisper tales they long to tell,
Unfolding slowly 'neath the sun,
Waiting for their time to come.

Gentle growth in quiet pose,
As nature's hand the beauty chose,
Seasons pass, and with each hour,
Patience proves to be a power.

In every bud that blooms at last,
Lies the wisdom of the past,
Time reveals the strength within,
As patience blossoms once again.

Respite in Repetition

In cycles bound with endless twine,
A rhythm steady, pulses fine.
With every beat, a chant so sweet,
A dance of time, in metronome's feet.

Ebb and flow of a ceaseless sea,
The ticking clock keeps company.
In loops we find a comfort's mind,
A soothing spell, with day entwined.

The heartbeat of the turning earth,
Marks a song of silent mirth.
In repetition, souls shall rest,
A lullaby for life's long quest.

The Eye of the Tempest

In the tempest's howling gale,
An eye whispers calm, steadfast and pale.
Chaos rages at the fringe,
While silence reigns at the center's hinge.

A core of peace midst the storm's wrath,
A path untrodden, a serene bath.
In the vortex, a still ballet,
Nature's contrast, in stark display.

Surrounded by a furious dance,
The tranquil heart holds a steadfast glance.
Amid the havoc, unswayed, unmoved,
The tempest's eye, eternally soothed.

Subtle Whispers Within

In the quietude of mind's retreat,
Silent murmurs, softly sweet.
Inner voice, amidst life's din,
Guides one's journey, from within.

Echoes of thoughts, gently heard,
Subtle whispers, without word.
In the soul's most secret den,
Voices chart the course of men.

Faint and hushed they may seem,
Yet they steer the waking dream.
Listen close, to what may win,
The subtle whispers, beneath the skin.

Pause Amidst the Pines

Within the woods of whispering pines,
Time's hurried footsteps fall behind.
A canopy's embrace, air's tender kiss,
Nature's chapel, graced with bliss.

Needles' carpet, an evergreen tide,
With each breath, the world's unhide.
In cloistered paths, birds' choir sings,
The forest's chorus, in rustling wings.

Here amidst the evergreen spires,
Life's fervor temporarily retires.
A pause from day's unending chase,
Within the pines, we find our grace.

Oasis of Calm

In the heart's secluded bower,
Quiet blooms the tranquil hour,
Gentle whispers call to rest,
Peace resides in nature's chest.

Amidst life's arid, dusty swirl,
Here the calm unfurls its curl,
Cooling thoughts that once were warm,
Sheltered from the stormy norm.

Palms sway soft in silent song,
Here, the tired spirit belongs,
Murmurs of the quiet breeze,
Soothe the mind with gentle ease.

In this isolated span,
Time's swift river slowly ran,
Breathing deep, the stress departs,
Oasis of the quiet hearts.

Lucidity Lake

Upon the lake of lucid thought,
Smooth reflections can be sought,
Clarity in water lies,
Beneath the open, azure skies.

Ripples carry gentle truth,
Echoes of my vanished youth,
The mirror of the soul so pure,
In still water, insights cure.

Across the surface, wisdom flies,
Skimming o'er the glass, it tries,
To tell of things deep and profound,
Where certainty is rarely found.

So, by the Lucidity Lake,
I sit and ponder, awake,
Each wave a lesson, a new take,
In serene thought, I partake.

Introspective Interlude

In solitude, the mind does speak,
Of whispers strong and prospects bleak,
An introspective quiet space,
Where echoes dwindle with no trace.

Uncertain shadows dance within,
A theater of thought begins,
The stage of self does brightly light,
The audience hidden from sight.

Each verse excavated deep,
From inner archives, long asleep,
Revealing fears and joys interred,
In silent interludes, I'm stirred.

This interlude of deep reflection,
Gives birth to paths of new direction,
Within the mind's secluded view,
I find the old and craft the new.

Pause for the Soul

Amid the rush, we seldom halt,
To ease the mind's relentless vault,
A pause for soul, a sacred space,
Can grant the heart a gentle grace.

We leave behind the noisy clatter,
In moments where such things don't matter,
Breathing out the weighty tolls,
Inhaling peace to soothe our souls.

A silent pause has much to say,
To those who choose to break away,
In quietude, we find the gold,
In life's loud market, rarely sold.

So take a pause, let silence reign,
And with it comes a softer gain,
For in the quiet, we console,
The whispers of the weary soul.

Clarity's Caress

Upon the dawn of thoughtful gaze,
In silence where the truths unlace,
Visions clear as crystal glass,
Shines the light of clarity's caress.

Whispers of wisdom softly tread,
Across the mind's vast open spread,
Each thought in pure light is dressed,
In the serene arms of clarity's caress.

Doubts dissipate in the morning sun,
The tangled knots come undone,
Surety sings in soothing press,
Under the touch of clarity's caress.

Eyes awake to radiant glow,
Life's complexion now in tow,
Future's path we can assess,
Guided by clarity's gentle caress.

The Breath's Ballet

Inhale begins the dancer's leap,
A silent waltz of rise and deep,
Each lung expands, a winged display,
To the rhythm of the breath's ballet.

Exhale pirouettes through the air,
A twirling release of worldly care,
Drifting feathers after play,
In the choreography of the breath's ballet.

Dance of life in constant flow,
Invisible thread only the heart can know,
A sweep of peace without dismay,
Moves within the breath's ballet.

With every cycle, grace is born,
New life is danced at each new morn,
The spirit sways without delay,
Throughout the masterpiece of breath's ballet.

Stillness Speaks

In the hush of the waking dawn,
The subtle stir of the day being born,
Quietude speaks without a word,
And in that silence, life is heard.

A tranquil pond, a mirrored scene,
Reflects the world's serene demesne,
Each ripple's speech is softly peaked,
Within the realm where stillness speaks.

Midst the chaos of the day,
There's a calm that does not sway,
A voice that the heart seeks,
In the solemn time when stillness speaks.

When the night descends, all is hushed,
Stars above in whispers brushed,
The cosmos in silence it shrieks,
Eloquent is the sound when stillness speaks.

The Mind's Mirror

In the mirror of the mind's eye,
Reflections cast of the inner I,
Thoughts and dreams pass in a smear,
Self-image drawn, crystal clear.

Memories etched on the pane of soul,
A gallery of life on an endless scroll,
The past and present in a dance appear,
Mirrored by the conscience, so near.

Imagination's figures, in shadows cast,
Upon the stage where the psyche's vast,
Each character plays their part sincere,
In the theater of the mind's mirror.

Look within, and you shall find,
A universe of the unique kind,
All that you hold dear,
Reflected back in the mind's mirror.

Lotus in the Lake of Thoughts

Atop the quiet mirrored sheen,
A lotus blooms pure and serene,
Thoughts like ripples come and go,
In the mind's lake, soft winds blow.

Beneath the surface, stems entwine,
The murky depths obscure the sign,
Within the mud, the roots embrace,
Holding fast to their nurturing base.

A petal opens to the sky,
Echoing a silent, heartfelt sigh,
The calm of water whispers true,
Reflecting fragments of our view.

In the stillness, peace is sought,
The lotus in the lake of thought,
As day embraces night's cool cloak,
In contemplation, life evokes.

Embers of Enlightenment

In the dark, a spark ignites,
A dance of truth that shuns the nights,
Glowing embers in the mind,
Guide the lost, the way they find.

Each a story, quietly told,
A piece of wisdom, ancient, bold,
Flaring bright as thoughts arise,
Casting shadows, cutting ties.

Warmth spreads through the heart's enclave,
Illuminating fears we braved,
The fire of knowing burns so bright,
Transforming souls with inner light.

So tend the flames with care and might,
Let not the fire of knowing smite,
For in each spark, there lies a choice,
To silence fear or give it voice.

Chasing the Inner Horizon

Beyond the veil of the waking eye,
Lies a horizon where dreams fly high,
In pursuit of the boundless sphere,
We chase the inner cosmos clear.

Adventures vast as the open heart,
Seeking the end, where do we start?
Through the mists of doubt, we run,
Until our inner and outer are one.

Horizons within, infinite and deep,
Hold secrets that the soul does keep,
Every moment a step towards the dawn,
A spirit's quest, tirelessly drawn.

We are the sailors of the mind's sea,
Chasing horizons where we are free,
With each breath, the chase is new,
Horizons within, ever-changing, true.

Whiff of Wisdom

Upon the breeze, a scent so slight,
A whiff of wisdom in the flight,
A fragrance that with truth does blend,
A wordless message, ear to lend.

Through ancient trees, it whispers clear,
Secrets of living without fear,
Each leaf a page, aged and wise,
Telling tales beneath the skies.

In untamed winds, advice does roam,
To every soul, it finds a home,
A silent mentor to those who heed,
A guide to plant enlightenment's seed.

Embrace the scent, wisdom's trace,
Let it lead to a higher place,
A whiff caught in life's grand dance,
Inhale deeply, give truth a chance.

Whispers of Tranquility

Beneath the willows' gentle sway,
A whispering breeze does lightly play.
Silent thoughts begin to weave,
In the cradle of peace, we softly grieve.

Upon a field of blooming heath,
Tranquility spreads its gentle sheath.
Stars above in quiet they twinkle,
In the hush of night, our worries shrinkle.

The moon casts forth its silvery glow,
Across the land, the calm winds blow.
Soft murmurs of the night prevail,
In each deep breath, our cares exhale.

Reflections in Still Water

In pools of mirror-like repose,
True beauty in reflection grows.
Gaze into the depths serene,
And see the world as it's rarely seen.

The ripples tell a tale so old,
Of sunlit glints and shadows bold.
In quietude, our minds take flight,
And dance with visions in the light.

Beneath the surface calm and clear,
The universe seems to draw near.
A moment caught in silent awe,
Reflects a world without a flaw.

Echoes of Peace

In the echo of the mountain's call,
A hush descends and covers all.
Through the valley, the whispers roam,
Carrying peace like a gentle home.

The songs of the forest in quiet ring,
Harmonies of serenity they bring.
Leaves rustle with a soft-sung grace,
Nature's choir fills the sacred space.

The world retires its weary pace,
In solitude, finds its embrace.
Amidst the stillness, echoes fly,
Bearing peace from the earth to the sky.

Resonance of Restfulness

In the silent vale of night, so deep,
Where moonbeams whisper secrets to keep,
Slumber's soft melody begins to play,
And draws the curtain on the bustling day.

Two by two, the stars align so bright,
Pledging solace until the morning light,
Each dream a note in this restful song,
In the heart's quiet orchestra, where they belong.

Gentle breezes hum through ancient trees,
Rustling leaves perform with effortless ease,
The resonance of restfulness fills the air,
Enveloping all in comfort, free from care.

In the realm where weary thoughts resign,
Under tranquil skies, peace becomes the sign,
As the world in hushed tones calmy rests,
Embraced by night's tender, soothing caress.

Inner Sanctum Symphony

Amidst the bustle, a silent core,
Where the inner sanctum symphony soars,
Strings of soul vibrate with pure intent,
A hidden concert of self-element.

Notes cascade in a cascade so clear,
Melodies that only the heart can hear,
In the mind's eye, they dance and they leap,
Synchronizing with the breaths so deep.

The rhythm of life, a pulse within,
Inner symphony's intimate din,
Echoes of essence, whispering truth,
Composing stanzas of eternal youth.

In solitude's embrace, the music swells,
A tale of harmony, each measure tells,
In this inner sanctum, quietly it plays,
The symphony of the soul, throughout the days.

Zenith of Zen

Atop the peak of serenity's mount,
By the stillness of the Zenith's fount,
Waters of calm ripple outward bound,
In the echoless void, peace is found.

Breath syncs with the timeless, gentle wind,
No beginning or end, where thoughts rescind,
Each inhale and exhale weaves through the void,
Pristine clarity, life is enjoyed.

In the garden where silence reigns supreme,
One transcends into a meditative dream,
Bathing in the Zenith's radiant gleam,
Reality dissolves into the stream.

Gilded in the soft glow of inner light,
The Zen pinnacle crafts visions so bright,
Harmony achieved, within the crest,
At the Zenith of Zen, souls find their rest.

Om's Vibrant Echo

In the silence profound and deep,
A single sound begins to creep,
Resonating with energy set free,
Om's vibrant echo flows through me.

Two worlds bridge with a hum so grand,
The universe nods on a gentle command,
All existence in harmony, dance,
The soul's vibrations, an endless trance.

Stars whisper secrets from above,
The echo pulsates with pure love,
Vibrant waves in the ether swim,
Connecting all life, limb to limb.

Majestic sound of the cosmos' dome,
Within every heartbeat, it finds a home,
Om's vibrant echo, the sacred sound,
In its resonance, we are all bound.

Between Heartbeats

In the space that lies between,
Heartbeats, silent and unseen,
Whispers of love softly tread,
On paths where wary feelings led.

A subtle pause, a moment's rest,
Between each beat within our chest,
Secrets told without a word,
In the quiet, unspoken truths are heard.

Two pulses in a rhythmic dance,
Creating life, by chance or glance,
In the stillness, time retreats,
A universe exists between heartbeats.

The ebb and flow of our desires,
Fuel the soul's undying fires,
Embracing life's sweet, fleeting treats,
In the sacred space between heartbeats.

The Ocean's Breath

Gentle waves caress the shore,
A soft sigh, the ocean's roar,
Each tide's retreat, a quiet plea,
Nature's breath, vast and free.

The pulse of water, in and out,
A world below we know not about,
Majestic blues, inhale, exhale,
The ocean's breath, a whispered tale.

Its rhythmic song, an ageless tune,
Under the gaze of sun and moon,
Waves that travel, never cease,
Whispering winds of watery peace.

Horizon's line, the meeting place,
Where sky and sea share a grace,
In every breath, the ocean's depth,
Endless stories that it has kept.

Canopy of Composure

Beneath the canopy of green,
A quiet composure, serene,
Leaves whisper in the gentle breeze,
Nature's calm, a quiet ease.

Branches arching, skyward high,
Sheltering dreams that to it lie,
A haven from life's chaotic spin,
Soothing the souls that rest within.

Tangled roots in the earth entwined,
Supporting each other, lives aligned,
A unity of strength unseen,
Beneath the tranquil canopy of green.

The world outside may thunder on,
But here, the turmoil is all gone,
Within this composure, souls repose,
Under the canopy, peace bestows.

Beneath the Buzzing

In fields where dandelions sway,
A gentle hum begins to play.
The bees commence their tireless buzz,
Nature's symphony, just because.

Beneath the buzzing, secrets hide,
In every flower, deep inside.
The pollen-laden treasure troves,
Busy workers in their droves.

They dance within the golden light,
From bloom to bloom, they take their flight.
A whispered drone beneath the sky,
Nature's endless lullaby.

While shadows stretch and hours wane,
The buzzing fades like whispered rain.
In hush of dusk, the dance slows down,
Beneath the stars, they wear their crown.

The Idle Idyll

Amidst the whisper of the breeze,
Where time slows to a tranquil tease,
The lazy river bends and winds,
In the idle idyll one finds.

The weeping willows gently sweep,
As dragonflies their vigils keep.
Reflecting skies so vast and still,
The world's own breath seems to distill.

No ticking clock dictating pace,
Just endless sky's soft-hued embrace.
The grass beneath, a cushioned seat,
Nature's own rhythm, slow and sweet.

The moments linger, gently blend,
Here, frantic hearts can start to mend.
The idyll whispers, calm and kind,
In nature's pause, true peace we find.

Gliding on Gossamer

Silent wings in pale moonlight,
Gliding through the tranquil night.
Threads of gossamer in the air,
Carry whispers of despair.

Yet upon such fragile thread,
Dreams and hopes are softly spread.
Floating high above our fears,
Gently drying hidden tears.

Grace within the slightest breeze,
Spirits loft with greatest ease.
Through the ether, silent roam,
Gossamer their guiding home.

Beneath the stars that softly gleam,
Gliding like a quiet dream.
The night's embrace, so tender, vast,
On gossamer, our cares are cast.

Finding the Void

In silence deep where thoughts recede,
A quiet void, the soul does need.
The cluttered mind seeks to avoid,
The peaceful realm, the tranquil void.

Beyond the noise of everyday,
Where chaos seems to fall away,
One finds a space so wide and clear,
The cosmic hush, the void draws near.

In emptiness, no fear or pain,
No tempest wild, no binding chain.
Just boundless calm where stress destroyed,
The heart's reprieve within the void.

So close your eyes, let go, let's start,
To find the void within your heart.
The journey inwards, softly poised,
To seek, embrace, the gentle void.

Unspoken Harmony

In silence, hearts beat a rhythmic dance,
Along the thread of an unseen trance,
Notes float, in the air, they sway and arc,
In the quiet, our souls speak without remark.

Whispers of the wind through an old oak tree,
Mirroring waves that chat with the sea,
Stars twinkle above in silent delight,
Unspoken harmony painting the night.

Movements in shadow, a delicate embrace,
Between two beings, in time and space,
Each glance a verse, each touch a chord,
In the hush, a silent symphony is scored.

The world speaks loud, yet we stand apart,
Communicating with the beat of our heart,
In the depths of silence where all is heard,
We find our peace, without a word.

Gentle Awakening

Dew-kissed leaves in the first light's gleam,
A world awakening from its emerald dream,
Sun whispers warmth on a sleepy land,
Day unfolds softly, as if by hand.

The gentlest touch of the morning's glow,
Calls to the flowers, 'It's time to grow',
Birdsong breaks, the new day's decree,
A proclamation of life, wild and free.

Under the horizon, a thin veil of mist,
Retreats from the sun's warm and tender kiss,
The sky, a canvas of pastel hues,
Announces the dawn, as day renews.

Each creature stirs in its time, its place,
Nature's symphony performs with grace,
With every sunrise, the world we see,
Awakes in beauty, awakes in glee.

Visions in the Void

In the void where the stars do not dare to shine,
Lie visions that thread the thinnest line,
Images flutter like a dreamer's thought,
In the abyss, the tapestries are wrought.

Eyes closed, I drift through the cosmic sea,
Bearing witness to what might or might not be,
Planets spin tales in silent decree,
In the great void, imagination roams free.

A dance of quasars, a nebula's birth,
Time weaves its tales, crafting the earth,
Portraits of worlds, both lost and found,
In the silent void, where wonders abound.

Through the vacuum, the void's gentle grace,
I find my spirit's interstellar place,
Where visions dwell, and the mind takes flight,
A universe hidden in the shroud of night.

Pondering the Infinite

Endless skies call to the thinker's mind,
Galaxies of questions, answers to find,
A vast expanse where thoughts can drift,
On the tides of the cosmos, our spirits lift.

At the edge of forever, where time seems still,
The philosopher's gaze drinks its fill,
Of stars strewn across the canvas, infinite,
Each point of light, a question implicit.

Universes swirl, a waltz of the divine,
A symphony of existence, elusive, sublime,
In the vast quiet, intellects roam,
Contemplating the heavens, calling it home.

Cosmic riddles whisper to those who seek,
Promising secrets for the brave, not meek,
In the arms of the infinite, ponder we must,
The origins of all, in the stardust.

The Mind's Quiet Corner

In the mind's most quiet corner,
Silent whispers softly linger,
Thoughts like leaves in gentle saunter,
In the calm, our spirits center.

Two by two, the worries pair off,
Leaving space for breath to sigh,
Serene waves of calm do takeoff,
Underneath the vast blue sky.

Shadows play on walls of thought,
Dancing with the light of peace,
Every battle once fought,
Finds in silence its release.

Restful haven, refuge sweet,
Cradling dreams in tender care,
In this corner, hearts may meet,
Finding solace, pure and rare.

Chimes of Clarity

When chimes of clarity softly ring,
Confusion fades, the mind takes wing,
Each tone's a note of inner truth,
A melody that guides the youth.

With every sound, a clear thought forms,
Transcending all the raging storms,
Ideas shine like stars at night,
Guiding us with their brilliant light.

The tolling bells of lucid dreams,
Cut through the fog, or so it seems,
Revealing paths once veiled in mist,
By clarity's sweet, gentle kiss.

In this chorus, thoughts align,
As chimes of clarity entwine,
A symphony of insight flows,
In its music, wisdom grows.

Unfurled Petals of Peace

Soft petals open to the dawn,
Unfurling peace that's been withdrawn,
Each bloom a testament to grace,
In their presence, calm takes place.

Steady heartbeats echo slow,
In the garden where peace does grow,
Petals whisper with the breeze,
Carrying serenity with ease.

Once tightly closed in self-defense,
Now blossom forth in confidence,
Unveiling tranquil shades of poise,
Amidst life's noise, a silent voice.

Here in the blooms, we come to find,
A quietude for heart and mind,
Petals of peace gently unfurled,
A soothing touch in a restless world.

Solitude's Symphony

Within the silence, music waits,
A symphony that contemplates,
The sound of self, so pure, profound,
In solitude, it's truly found.

Each note a step along a trail,
Where whispered breezes tell their tale,
A melody in each deep breath,
In solitude, we dance with death.

It's not a sound of loneliness,
But richer chords that soothe and bless,
The spirit's song, so clear, resolute,
In symphony with each muted flute.

Embrace the quiet, let it teach,
The lessons only silence can reach,
In solitude's symphony so bold,
We find a harmony in our soul.

Solace of the Sunrise

In quietude, the dawn doth break,
With tints of blush on heaven's lake,
As whispers of the morn arise,
The world awakes to tranquil skies.

A soft embrace of amber light,
Erases remnants of the night,
Each ray a painter's stroke of grace,
A masterpiece in time and space.

The sky, a canvas broad and bright,
Illuminates the world's delight,
As solace wraps in warmth's embrace,
The sunrise gives the heart its pace.

Beneath the gaze of morning's bloom,
All fears and sorrows find their tomb,
For in the dawn's new splendid guise,
We find the strength to open eyes.

Channeling Chiaroscuro

Between the light, the shadow plays,
A dance of dusk and breaking days,
Contrasts blend where edges meet,
The chiaroscuro's bittersweet.

In art, a realm of half-tone thrives,
Where brilliance with the muted vies,
Each stroke, the balance of the hue,
Creates a scene both false and true.

The dark defines the edge of light,
A symphony in black and white,
The depth of night, the crest of morn,
In juxtaposed hues are born.

Embrace the spectrum wide and vast,
No moment shades the previous cast,
In life's own canvas, find your glow,
Channel the light, let shadows go.

Temple of Thought

In solitude's sacred shrine,
Within the temple of the mind,
Thoughts weave like tapestries untold,
In intricate patterns, bold and old.

Beneath the dome of consciousness,
Ideas frolic and convalesce,
Each notion a prayer, silently cast,
In the cathedral of the vast.

Transcend the mortal, fleeting fleet,
Within this space, the soul's retreat,
A cloistered corner, still and fraught,
With the gentle echoes of thought.

Here we ponder life's great plot,
Our inner questions twist and knot,
The temple's wisdom, always sought,
In sacred silence, answers brought.

Equanimity Echoes

In gentle streams of silent thought,
Where mind's deep peace is freely sought,
An echo forms of tranquil might,
In balanced dance of day and night.

Beneath the tumult and the noise,
A steady heart, its beat, poise,
Through storm and tempest stands unmoved,
In equanimity, approved.

The soul's soft whisper, clear and true,
In each ordeal finds its cue,
A harmony amidst life's throes,
In serenity, it glows.

Amidst the clamor of the fray,
Still waters reflect a quieter way,
The echoes of composure sing,
And to the mind, its peace they bring.

Sabbath of the Psyche

A pause within, the psyche's rest,
From toil and tumult, a silent quest,
A space to breathe, reflect, be whole,
A sabbath day for the wearied soul.

The mind unwinds in stillness sweet,
In this retreat, the heart does beat,
A tempo slow, a measured tread,
On softened paths, we're gently led.

Time's relentless march suspends,
As inward gaze on self attends,
Renewed in spirit, clear in sight,
The psyche's sabbath bathes in light.

A day apart from worldly cares,
An inner peace that time repairs,
The mind's own haven, safe and sound,
Where thoughts of calm and hope are found.

The Quiet Quest

In silence deep, the quest begins,
A journey inward, free of sins,
In quietude, the soul's soft call,
Eclipses doubt, and hushes all.

The gentle search for inner truth,
A voyage ripe with verdant youth,
Through forests of the inner scape,
To lands untouched by worldly shape.

Whispers of wisdom in the air,
Answers found in stillness there,
The quiet quest leads on and on,
Until the clamoring is gone.

Each step upon this hallowed ground,
The seeker's heart with peace is crowned,
In inner realms, the truth is guest,
And in the quiet, we find our quest.

Beyond the Buzz

Beyond the drone of daily grind,
The buzz, the rush that binds the mind,
There lies a realm, serene, profound,
Where truth and clarity abound.

Turn off the noise, step through the haze,
Escape the maze of hurried days,
To find a place that's pure and still,
Beyond the buzz, a tranquil thrill.

In whispers of the rustling leaves,
In the calm breath that evening heaves,
There's knowledge that eludes the fuss,
A world apart, beyond the buzz.

So seek the silence, deep and wise,
Beyond the noise that blinds our eyes,
And in that hush, you'll find, because,
All life speaks soft, beyond the buzz.

Pulse of the Infinite

In the void where stars are spun,
Eternal beats, a distant drum,
A cosmic heart, forever young,
Pulse of the Infinite, unsung.

Vast emptiness, yet full of life,
Harmony's threads, through dark and light,
Each beat resounds, clear and finite,
In the endless dance of night.

Galaxies twirl in silent song,
Time's river carries them along,
An orchestra to which we belong,
Pulse of the Infinite, strong.

Flowing through the velvet skies,
Whispering truths behind the lies,
A rhythm felt with inner eyes,
In the Pulse of the Infinite, we rise.

Whirlwind to Whisper

Fierce winds arise from silent breeze,
A dance of chaos, souls to seize,
Whirlwind's might, trees bow with ease,
Nature's maelstrom nobody flees.

Yet in the eye, a tranquil span,
From raging storm to calm began,
A moment's peace amidst the plan,
Whirlwind falls to whisper, as if on ban.

The tempest's roar fades to a hush,
Swift is the change, a gentle brush,
Echoes of silence, in the flush,
From Whirlwind to Whisper, the world's soft crush.

In whispered tones, the Earth doth speak,
Of strength in stillness, not in the weak,
A balance sought by those who seek,
From Whirlwind to Whisper, a truth unique.

Dancing with Tranquility

In solitude's embrace, we find,
A dance with peace, of tranquil kind,
Gentle steps, left behind,
With every move, align the mind.

In stillness, swaying trees conspire,
To teach the art of soft desire,
The rustling leaves like quiet lyre,
Dancing with Tranquility, aspire.

Beneath the moon's soft silver glow,
Where shadows cast and breezes blow,
Serenity's rivers ever flow,
In dance, our quiet hearts we show.

With every breath, a silent plea,
To waltz with calm serenity,
Harmony's silent symphony,
Dancing with Tranquility, we're free.

Reflections in the Mind's Mirror

In the mirror of the mind we gaze,
Past and future, in a haze,
stories old, and thoughts ablaze,
Reflections twist in endless ways.

Through the glass of time now seen,
Memories of what has been,
Mixed with dreams of worlds unseen,
Enigmatic, yet serene.

A pool of thought, deep and vast,
Mirroring a shadowed past,
Images that hold us fast,
In mind's mirror, they're cast.

On the surface, ripples spread,
Echoes of the life we've led,
In the mind's mirror, softly tread,
Reflections of the soul, unsaid.

The Mind's Monastery

In the cloister of my thoughts, so deep,
Where secrets and desires are kept,
Echoes of silence pave the stones,
And solitude sits on its earthen thrones.

Within these walls, a calm retreat,
The mind's own heart skips a beat,
Meditations swirl in a gentle dance,
While the soul looks on in a tranquil trance.

Candles of wisdom flicker and glow,
The chime of insight begins to grow,
A tapestry of knowledge unfurls,
As serenity around me twirls.

The abbey bells of my inner chant,
Ring out fears, in quiet recant,
In this monastery, calm musters,
Where the mind's peace softly flutters.

Unraveled Rhythms

Beneath the moon's silent croon,
Lies a melody, out of tune,
Strings of the heart, gently plucked,
In the symphony of life, now amuck.

Notes scattered across the sky,
On wings of wind, they say goodbye,
The harmony of the day comes undone,
Under the watchful eye of the setting sun.

The tempo slows to the beat of time,
As twilight ushers the night's prime,
Stars twinkle in rhythmic rhyme,
While the universe hums in sublime.

Echoes of the day, softly fade,
Night's serenade is gently laid,
In unraveling rhythms, we find grace,
And in the quiet, a resting place.

Dawning of Detachment

The first light of dawn peeks with care,
Across the sky, so fresh and fair,
The shroud of night, gently shed,
As new thoughts break their tethered thread.

Clouds part ways for clarity's rise,
As the soul lets go of heavy ties,
In the hush of morn, I find release,
In the dawning of detachment, sweet peace.

The horizon blushes with gentle hope,
The spirit climbs a higher slope,
The chains of yesterday softly fracture,
In the morning light, a new chapter.

Embrace the calm, the quiet so bold,
Letting go of the grip from the old,
The sun ascends, heart's woes retract,
In the daybreak, I embrace the act.

Heartbeat of Hush

In the heartbeat of hush, the world's at rest,
A silent symphony beats in my chest,
The rush and roar of the day take flight,
Leaving behind the tender night.

Stars pulsate in the quiet sky,
Their ancient glow, a soft lullaby,
A cosmos held in a single beat,
While the earth beneath whispers discreet.

In the realm of calm, time stands still,
The heart listens for what the noise will kill,
Every breath a hushed rhythm plays,
And the night's caress softly stays.

Each whisper of wind, a soothing touch,
In the world's embrace, we aren't much,
Yet in the heartbeat of hush, we trust,
In the silent orchestra of the dusk.

Inward Voyage

To delve inside the soul's deep well,
In search of truths too rare to tell.
Each whispered echo sounds a bell
Inviting minds to inward dwell.

Beneath the surface, secrets sleep,
In shadows vast, in canyons steep.
The heart's compass, in silence, leapt
To find the course that spirit kept.

With every step the journey wanes,
For every thought is a chain.
Yet in the depths, the still remains
Become the keys to break the chains.

The voyage inward goes not far,
Yet reaches past the furthest star.
In quietude, we find our span,
The universe within a man.

Breath by Breath

Inhale the dawn, the gentle light,
Exhale the shadows of the night.
Each breath a voyage, faint and bright,
A silent mentor in plain sight.

With every rise, the chest expands,
On unseen shores, with golden sands.
A cycle shared by all life's strands,
United by the air's commands.

Breath by breath, we build our days,
On pillars of mist, in myriad ways.
Through storms within, the calmness stays,
A guiding wind through life's vast maze.

The simple act, the living art,
A meditation of the heart.
In every end is just the start;
From every finish, we depart.

Still Waters Within

Beneath the ripple, there's a calm,
A hidden place, a soothing balm.
An inner lake, so still, so warm,
A refuge from the outer storm.

We float upon the silent wave,
In quiet mind's embrace we're saved.
Each worry we let go, to brave
The deeper peace we seek to crave.

The surface tension breaks with ease,
As breath and thought like clouds do cease.
The mirrored mind reflects pure peace,
In stillness all the turmoils lease.

Turn inward to the tranquil deep,
Where secrets of serenity sleep.
In such quietude, we reap
A harvest calm, for soul to keep.

Zenith of Calm

At the zenith of calm, on the peak of repose,
Where the clutter of life finds its gentlest close.
Serene thoughts ascend, there in balance they teem,
The pinnacle's point, where the tranquil dream.

No storm may reach where the clear minds soar,
Above the din, the worldly roar.
In solitude's castle, bolt the door,
And bask in peace, forevermore.

Here, atop the silent crest,
Where chaos finds its final rest.
The soul's unrest is laid to test,
And yields to calm, as a welcomed guest.

The zenith of calm, a summit's breath,
Away from life's unending quest.
Here time's tumult meets its death,
And in this hush, we find our zest.

The Pulse of Hush

In silence profound, the night takes its vow,
Echoing softly, the world sleeps now.
The pulse of hush, beats life's gentle rush,
In the stillness, nature speaks, cajole.

Cloaked in darkness, the earth holds her breath,
Quiet whispers traverse, secrets bequeath.
The rhythm of calm, in the night's soft palm,
Under starlit skies, tranquility's role.

The murmur of leaves, a hushed serenade,
Under the moon's glow, the end of day fades.
The heart's soft whisper, in silence, crisper,
Bearing the soul's weight, the silence consoles.

Time's quiet footfalls in the corridors of dusk,
Moments suspended, as if in a husk.
The hush is imbued, with peace not eluded,
In the quiet, the world finds its muse.

Tapestries of Thought

My mind, a loom, thoughts intertwine and weave,
Patterns emerge from the dreams I conceive.
A tapestry rich, with color and stitch,
Picturing moments, in memory's sleeve.

Ideas spin gold in the weaver's hand,
Silken threads of logic, understand.
Complex and fine, a design divine,
Spreading across consciousness like sands.

Threads of emotion, the warp and weft,
Woven through time, in the weaver's deft.
A portrait so vast, of the present and past,
In life's fabric, each thread is a gift.

This tapestry hangs in the mind's quiet hall,
A patchwork of dreams, transcendental call.
Eternal and bright, depth mistaken for height,
On thought's loom, the heart of us all.

Whistling Winds of Wisdom

Whistling winds of wisdom, whispered words,
Serenading minds like unseen birds.
Carrying tales from times far and wide,
In their melodies, truth and lies reside.

Sweeping o'er the hills, through the trees,
Rustling the silence, as they please.
Each gust a story, each breeze a page,
In the air, the script of every age.

These zephyrs hum with ancestral voice,
In their ancient knowledge, we rejoice.
Every leaf's dance, each bending frond,
Echoes wisdom, of which we're fond.

Listen to the wind, the sage's song,
In its rhythm, we are strong and belong.
Through whispered chants, in the listening skies,
The winds of wisdom eternally rise.

Symphony of Solitude

In the quietude of solitude's arms,
I find a symphony of tranquil charms.
The heart's solo pulse, in vastness hums,
An orchestra of silence, cleverly strums.

The melody plays in a solo flight,
Sweeping through day and serenading night.
No crowds to cheer, no applause to plead,
Just the sound of self, in which I heed.

In solitude's grasp, the mind does clear,
And the soul's voice is all I hear.
Notes pure and true rise in the air,
A composition of inner care.

Thus, I sit, audience to my core,
In solitude's symphony, I explore.
With each breath, a note resonates new,
In this silent music, life's cue, I pursue.

Restful Ruminations

In the silence of the night so deep,
Under the sky where the willows weep,
My mind to the cosmos quietly creeps,
In the tranquil hours before the sleep.

In this stillness, thoughts begin to steep,
Like tea leaves in a cup held with keep,
Memories and dreams in a layered heap,
The heart whispers secrets it can't speak.

Moonlight casts a glow, soft and replete,
On hopes and desires that in shadows peep,
Between the conscious and slumber's seat,
Restful ruminations in their retreat.

The night's calm breath, a soothing balm,
As thoughts meander in silence calm,
In this quiet, a world of charm,
The soul finds solace and healing salm.

The Tender Pause

A gentle hush betwixt the chaos,
Moments of calm, the tender pause,
When life's loud storms momentarily dost thaw,
And time's frenetic ticking softly saus.

In this brief breath, the racing heart slows,
With the flutter of wings, a lone bird crows,
In reflection deep, the mind bestows,
A tranquil space where quietude grows.

Eyes catch the drifting cotton cloud,
The wind's sweet whisper, not too loud,
Serenity wrapped like a soft shroud,
The soul's respite from life's unbowed crowd.

In the tender pause, our essence meets,
With the world's rhythm in silent greets,
A soothing lull that gently treats,
The weary spirit with restful feats.

Murmur of Moments

Soft whispers in the hallway of time,
Echoes of the past, like bells that chime,
Each tick and tock, a subtle rhyme,
In the murmur of moments, we find prime.

Life's fleeting winks, caught in a glance,
As the hours and minutes quietly dance,
A hidden cadence amidst the advance,
Of seconds that weave the day's trance.

Breath to breath, a seamless flow,
In each small instance, the future's sow,
A chain of instants, a tender bough,
Carrying the weight of the here and now.

In every heartbeat, a story untold,
Of love and loss, new and old,
In the murmuring moments, our tales are rolled,
Silent and speaking, brave and bold.

Time in Suspension

Caught in a web where the clock stands still,
A motionless sphere, the world at will,
Each minute stretches, a time to instill,
Moments breathless, with a chill thrill.

Suspended high, above the fray,
Detached from the night, removed from the day,
Floating in an endless gray,
Where thoughts and dreams might softly lay.

Above the rush, the human race,
A quiet void, a tranquil space,
Freedom from time's tight embrace,
In this limbo, find a gentle grace.

Within this bubble where seconds cease,
The mind can wander, at ease, at peace,
And as the minutes slowly release,
We savor time in suspension's lease.

Auroras of the Soul

Whispers of light in the darkened sky,
A tapestry of dreams begins to untie.
Ethereal dancers in hues so bright,
Waltzing with stars through the eternal night.

Cascading colors, a celestial flow,
Chasing the darkness with an iridescent glow.
Each shimmering wave a silent decree,
Of the boundless beauty inside you and me.

In the solace of night, where thoughts rove free,
Auroras of the soul dance quietly.
Glimpses of wonder that internally dwell,
In shades of emotions that wordlessly tell.

A mirage of peace in the silent expanse,
Soul's deepest yearnings given a chance.
To ignite the spirit with inner light's grace,
A journey through cosmos, a transcendental chase.

The Art of Stillness

In the quietude of the dimming day,
The world slows down and peels away.
Beneath the hush, a tranquil art,
A sanctuary for the restless heart.

Soft whispers of the slowing breath,
An inner realm with no touch of death.
Pondering life with a gentle gaze,
Finding the calm in the everyday maze.

The stillness speaks in a silent tongue,
Tales of time since the world was young.
Harnessing peace among the rush,
A symphony heard in the softest hush.

Embrace the pause, the sacred lull,
Where clarity's stream flows deep and full.
In the art of stillness, find your ease,
As serenity blossoms in the quiet breeze.

Mindful Musings at Midnight

In the depth of night's embrace,
The mind stirs from its resting place.
Contemplations rise, bold and unfiltered,
On a canvas of silence, thoughts are splintered.

Shadows play on the walls of the mind,
A theatre of memories, uniquely aligned.
Questions of existence quietly unfold,
In this introspective warmth, despite the cold.

There's a beauty found in night's dark hours,
Where thoughts bloom like nocturnal flowers.
Embracing the peace, so rare and so fleeting,
Tunes of the heart and mind softly meeting.

Midnight muses on life's grand expanse,
A dance with fate, a serendipitous chance.
In the still of the dark, insights are born,
A tapestry woven until the morn.

Twilight's Tranquil Muse

Twilight whispers to the closing day,
A final curtain, a peaceful ballet.
Horizon glows with a fading light,
Harbinger of the approaching night.

Stars prick the sky in a gentle tease,
A prelude to the evening's ease.
Twilight's muse in her silent mirth,
Cradles the transitions of the earth.

A soft murmur of the dwindling sun,
A day's end, another night begun.
In the calm, there stirs a deep reflection,
Nature's lullaby, a quiet perfection.

Surrender to the dusky, tranquil call,
As dusk enfolds, a comforting shawl.
In the tender grip of night's soft embrace,
Find solace in twilight's gentle grace.

Silence in the Garden

In the garden's hush at dawn's soft light,
Petals dew-kissed, shimmering bright.
Ancient trees stand guard in silent might,
While morning unfurls its tender plight.

The air so still, nature's mute refrain,
Sunbeams dance on leaves after rain.
Butterflies twirl in a silent ballet,
In this tranquil place, time slips away.

Not a whisper stirs the solemn peace,
As all of life's clamors seem to cease.
The garden's silence, a sacred lease,
Under its spell, all troubles release.

The Whisper of Serenity

There's a whisper on the wind, a gentle call,
Serenity's touch that befalls us all.
In the quiet moment of a starlit night,
The soul finds calm, bathed in silvery light.

Gentle murmurs of the rippling stream,
Speak of peace found in a dream.
Leaves that rustle with a hush,
Compose the world's serene, soft blush.

In every breath, the whisper grows,
Through the meadows where the river flows.
Embrace the hush, the tranquil scene,
As serenity whispers, silent and serene.

Solitude's Embrace

In solitude's embrace, I find my space,
The world recedes with a measured pace.
Alone, not lonely, in my refuge so serene,
With only thoughts as companions, keen.

The silent songs that solitude sings,
The peace and clarity that it brings.
In the stillness, reflections arise,
Whispering truths, no need for disguise.

Through solitude's door, I step inside,
To confront myself, nowhere to hide.
Embraced in quiet, I come to see,
The strength in stillness, the power to be free.

Breathe In, Breathe Out

Breathe in deeply, inhale the peace,
Let go of turmoil, find sweet release.
With each slow breath, feel the bind loosen,
Embrace the calm, let new life begin.

Breathe out slowly, expel the strife,
Rhythms of breathing, echoes of life.
Cares fall away like leaves from a tree,
In every exhale, set your spirit free.

Inhale the future, hope's gentle kiss,
Exhale the past, the moments amiss.
The simple mantra for life's devout,
Forever enduring: breathe in, breathe out.

Hushed Enlightenment

In silent shades of ambient light,
Beneath the stars, pure and bright,
Wisdom perches on the night,
In whispers of the quiet sight.

Within the calm, insight grows,
Where silence blooms and knowledge flows,
Hushed tones of enlightenment shows,
The path where tranquil thought bestows.

Beneath the moon's serene discourse,
Nature yields its guiding force,
In gentle waves, without remorse,
Presents the course without coerce.

Upon the mind's soft shores it crests,
Where silent echos fill the quests,
Each wave of thought at peace and rests,
In hushed enlightenment, it invests.

Murmurs of the Mind

In the depth of thought's embrace,
Echoes stir, a subtle trace,
Murmurs rise from a hidden place,
Crafting mazes in silent space.

Whispers weave through mental halls,
Softly tread on memory's walls,
Dialogue that gently calls,
With each hushed echo that befalls.

Conversations with the self,
Books of musings pulled off the shelf,
Internal murmurs, a quiet wealth,
In mind's domain, the self does delve.

Shadows speak in hushed tones low,
Rustling ideas that ebb and flow,
Murmurs grow and softly glow,
In mind's endless, bustling show.

Drifting Through Thought

Adrift upon the thought's great sea,
Ideas float, wild and free,
Billowing sails in the mind's decree,
Horizons of inner sanctity.

Waves of concepts rise and fall,
Carried by the cerebral squall,
Upon imagination, they call,
Creating stories to enthrall.

Through the currents of the brain,
Navigating the introspective plane,
Seeking truths we strive to explain,
While in thought, we remain.

Mists of musings softly drift,
Through synaptic canyons swift,
In this eternal mental shift,
Ideas through the fog they lift.

The Tranquil Trail

Upon a path serene and clear,
Footsteps tread without a fear,
Nature's whispers, the soul to cheer,
On the tranquil trail, peace draws near.

Canopied by leafy arms,
Soothed by nature's calming balms,
The forest cloaks in loving charms,
The heart within, it gently calms.

Gentle brooks with murmured tales,
Winding paths, in light or gales,
The tranquil trail never fails,
To heal the spirit that it hails.

In silent communion with the earth,
We find a sense of quiet mirth,
On trails where peace is given birth,
We walk in solace, embracing worth.

Harmonious Solace

In whispers of the rustling leaves,
A melody of tranquil ease,
The zephyr hums in gentle tone,
A harmonious solace, fully grown.

Amidst the chaos, softly it lies,
A stream of peace beneath the skies,
In every breath, a lullaby,
That soothes the soul when spirits are high.

The dance of light on meadows wide,
Where shadows play, and sunbeams glide,
Each daisy bows in graceful poise,
As nature sings with silent voice.

The twilight brings its tender muse,
With hues of pink, subtle blues,
In solace found within the night,
Until the dawn brings morning light.

Conscious Stillness

In the quiet mind, thoughts lay bare,
A stillness breathes the cool night air,
Serene and poised, the heart takes heed,
To the soft murmur of the reed.

Stars twinkle in the conscious sky,
While the world sleeps, and night birds fly,
A moment's pause, a silent crest,
In the hush of darkness, souls find rest.

Moments fleet, time quietly stolen,
In the depth of night, whispers golden,
Every beat, a calm rhythm feels,
In the web of stillness, silence heals.

The mind's expanse, vast and deep,
Where secrets and shadows gently weep,
Untethered dreams in the quiet sprawl,
Conscious stillness, embracing all.

Contemplation Canopy

Beneath the canopy of thought,
Where contemplation threads are wrought,
The mind explores with earnest leap,
Unveiling truths that lie so deep.

Ideas flutter like leaves in wind,
Forming patterns, ever pinned,
To the vast tapestry of the mind,
In infinite weave, they're intertwined.

Each notion blooms, a flower's grace,
In the garden of cognitive space,
With petals of insight, soft and pure,
Nurturing growth that shall endure.

The shaded grove of inner quest,
Where solace meets the heart's behest,
Under the contemplation canopy,
Lies the serene orchard of discovery.

Serene Horizons

Upon the brink of dawn's embrace,
The sky paints blush on night's chaste face,
Horizons stretch in silent speech,
Serene as far as thoughts can reach.

The sun ascends with golden thread,
In quiet hues of rose and red,
It weaves through clouds in soft reprieve,
Infinite canvas it does conceive.

Gentle waves of light unfurl,
Over a world that's yet to swirl,
In this hour, calm and kind,
Horizons touch the tranquil mind.

Breathe in the day, fresh and new,
Where sky meets earth in calming hue,
Promise etched in morning's glow,
Serene horizons, endless flow.

The Kinetic Pause

In the rush of the whirring world still,
Pausing heart 'midst the endless fray.
Time hesitates on its relentless drill,
In the midst of hustle, we find our way.

Beneath the canopy of cosmos wide,
Breath by breath, the urgent pace slows.
In tranquility's arms, we briefly hide,
The kinetic pause, where serenity grows.

The dance of life momentarily at rest,
Reflection's gaze through the vibrant din.
In the stillness, finding the quest,
Not in the noise, but the quiet within.

Hurried thoughts now wander loose,
In the pause, the spirit dares to rise.
From every break, new paths deduce,
In every end, a new beginning lies.

The Sage's Silence

Spoken word, the sage forsakes,
Answers found in silent lakes.
Wisdom hidden in quiet breath,
Revelations beyond life and death.

Mountaintop, devoid of sound,
Truths untold, secrets abound.
In the hush, the universe speaks,
Silence holds the truths we seek.

Resonance of a calm mind's plea,
Harmony held in the quiet sea.
Beyond the clamor, peace ascends,
In silence, the shattered spirit mends.

Ears attuned to the whispering wind,
Sage's silence, where insights begin.
The muted chant of the world's heart,
Silent knowledge to impart.

Veil of the Visceral

Veiling glances, soul's raw cry,
Unseen passions that fly on high.
Glimpses of the true desires,
Flickering of the inner fires.

Hidden depth, emotional lore,
The heart's secrets behind the door.
Touch of fate, tender and visceral,
The silent ache transferable.

Danced emotions in the dark,
Whispered longings leave their mark.
Underneath, the rawness weaves,
Visceral veil, the spirit heaves.

Torn between the seen and felt,
A life in candid moments dwelt.
Deep within, the truth unfurls,
In the visceral veil, authenticity swirls.

Passage to Peace

Gentle whispers in the night's embrace,
Leading to a tranquil, hallowed space.
Within each breath, a silent plea,
In the passage to peace, the soul flies free.

Quietude's path, softly tread,
To the haven where fears are shed.
Weight of the world, gently release,
Drifting forth, in search of peace.

Through tempests and turmoil, a steady course,
The heart navigates to its source.
In calm passage, turmoil will cease,
Harmony found in the journey to peace.

Each step taken, a solemn vow,
To seek serenity, here and now.
At passage's end, conflicts decrease,
In peace's embrace, we find our release.

www.ingramcontent.com/pod-product-compliance
Lightning Source LLC
LaVergne TN
LVHW020421070526
838199LV00003B/231